For my children,
May you always remember
my love.

Snow means one of their favorite times of the year.

A time of renewal when the nights are long. A time to create while we are all inside.

Creating ornaments with salt dough is such a blast.

On the fourth day of Yule, Mommy talks about winter deities and the spirits of Yule as they all bake cookies together.

On the sixth day of Yule, the family exchanges homemade gifts they made, and shares what they appreciate about each other.

On the eighth day of Yule, the children learn the power of giving as they choose a toy to donate to children in need.

On the tenth day of Yule, the children learn about other holidays celebrated around the world during this time.

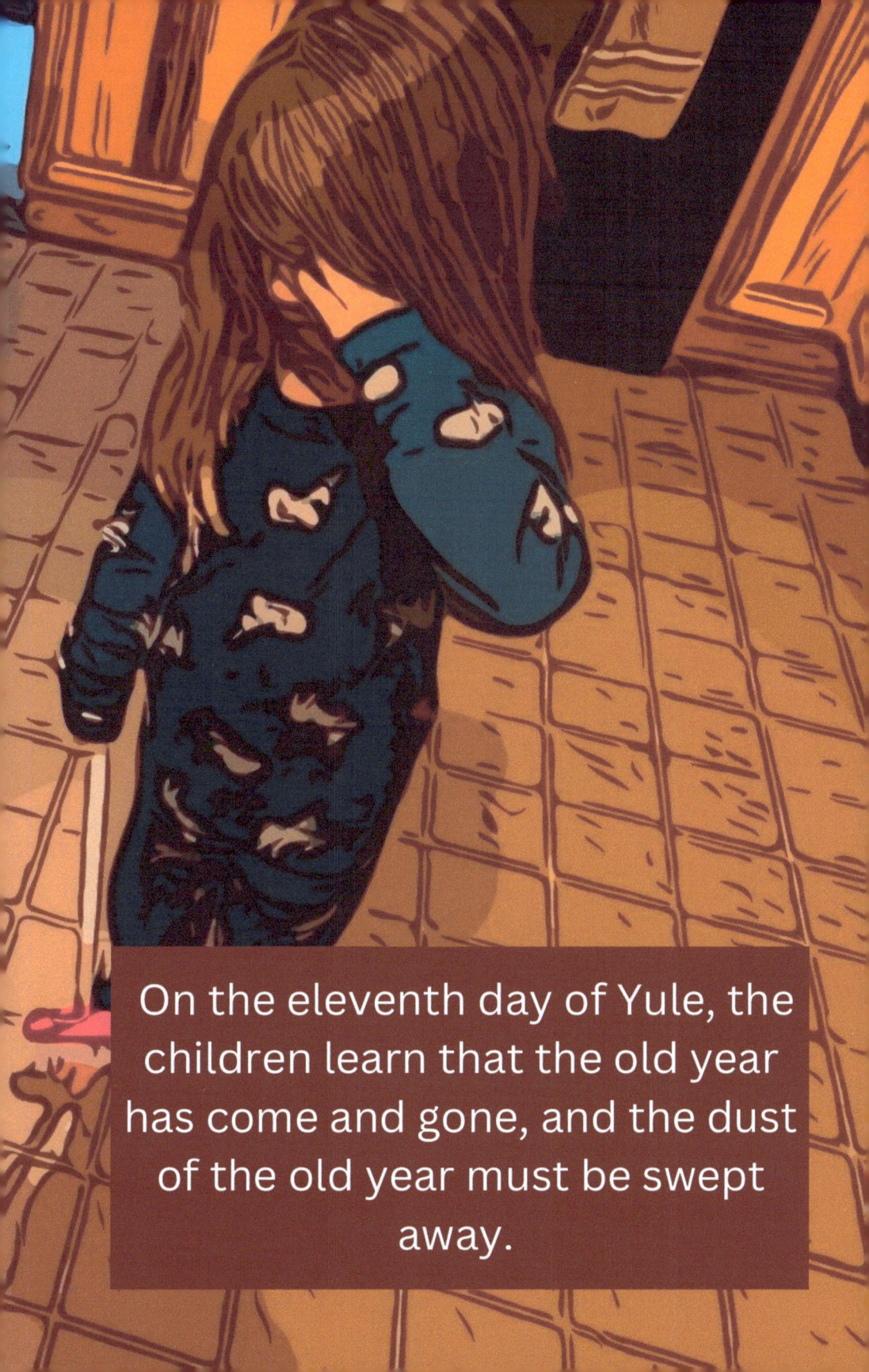

On the eleventh day of Yule, the children learn that the old year has come and gone, and the dust of the old year must be swept away.

On the twelfth day of yule, the children are asked what they wish to come in the new year.

Mommy writes those wishes on bay leaves and casts them into the Yule fire.

www.ingramcontent.com/pod-product-compliance
Lightning Source LLC
Chambersburg PA
CBHW041813040426
42450CB00001B/25